Smart Solutions

Program Authors

Connie Juel, Ph.D.

Jeanne R. Paratore, Ed.D.

Deborah Simmons, Ph.D.

Sharon Vaughn, Ph.D.

PEARSON
Scott Foresman

Glenview, Illinois
Boston, Massachusetts
Chandler, Arizona
Upper Saddle River, New Jersey

ISBN-13: 978-0-328-45281-1
ISBN-10:   0-328-45281-5

2 3 4 5 6 7 8 9 10 V011 14 13 12 11 10
CC1

Smart Solutions

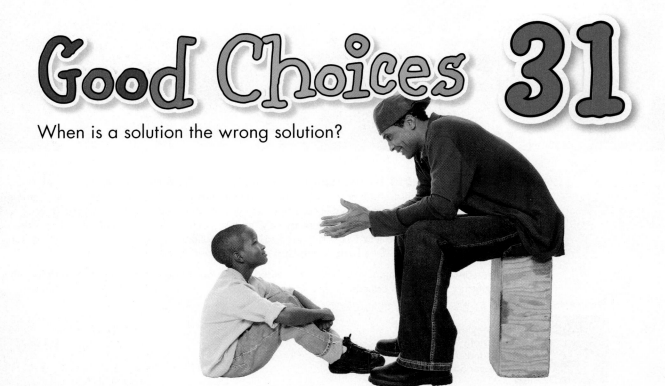

Animal Answers

Contents

Animal Answers

Words 2 the Wise

Animals survive because they adapt to their environments. How do animals adapt? As you read you will learn the **animal answers.**

ANIMAL SURVIVAL

A possum plays dead. Other animals leave it alone.

A rabbit eats in the dark. It is hard for other animals to spot it.

A worm hides. It is safe from birds.

How do animals survive? Like you, they must have a safe place to live. They must rest and get enough to eat and drink. But they must also escape from animals that can harm them. They must not let other animals eat them for lunch!

How can animals do this? Here are some tricks.

8

A horned lizard blends in with rocks and sand.

A kit fox hunts.

BLENDING IN

A kit fox is hunting for lunch. Will it spot the reptile hidden in the rocks and sand? Not if this reptile is very still. This reptile blends in with its environment. The fox will mistake it for rocks and sand!

A crab has a hard shell.

HARD SHELLS

Click, click, click. A crab darts across sharp rocks. It is not hard to spot. It does not blend in.

What helps this animal escape harm? It has a hard shell. This special part protects it from the sharp bills of gulls and other birds. This hard shell helps it survive.

A blue shark hunts.

Fish swim in a school.

SAFETY IN NUMBERS

A blue shark glides through dark water. It smells fish—a nice snack. These fish do not blend in or have shells. So how can they escape this hunting shark? They can swim close together in a group. Then they look like one big fish that is too big to gulp!

Did You See What I Saw?

by Jerod Arden

Sizes, shapes, and colors help animals blend in with their environments. This protects them.

Flip. Flop. Did you see what I saw?

I spotted a rock in the water. It is close to shore. But it is not a rock. It is a stonefish. It has dark skin and bumps like some rocks. Which is the fish? Which is the rock?

Twist. Slide. Did you see what I saw?

I spotted a vine. This vine is smart. It is the vine snake. It is long and thin. It lives in the forest and hides in trees. It swings from side to side. This snake looks like a tree vine. Can you pick out the vine and pick out the snake?

Hop. Skip. Jump. Did you see what I saw?

I spotted a tree frog. This green tree frog lives in damp, or wet, places. It lives in forests that get lots of rain. The tree frog sits in trees and rests on branches. It can adapt by changing its colors very fast. Quick! Did you spot the tree frog?

The tree frog changes color when it is cold out. It changes to a dark shade of green. This makes it warm. But when it is hot out, it changes to a shade that is not dark. This helps it from getting hot. Can you spot the frog when it is warm? Can you spot it when it is not?

Scamper. Dash. Did you see what I saw?

I spotted a bug. This bug is the stinkbug. It lives in shrubs.* Some stinkbugs are black and some are green. This stinkbug is black. It is not as big as a green stinkbug. Can you spot the black stinkbug when it blends?

**shrubs* bushes

Here is a stinkbug that is green. It can get as long as one inch in size. Its shape is like the blade* of a plant. Can you trace the shape of the plant in this picture? Now trace the shape of the stinkbug. Are they almost the same?

blade flat, wide part of a leaf

Quick. Slick. Did you see what I saw?

I spotted an Arctic fox. The Arctic fox lives in the far North. When it is winter this fox is white. Can you find the Arctic fox?

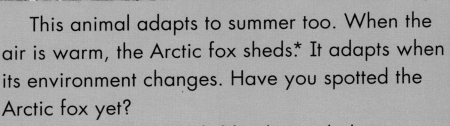

This animal adapts to summer too. When the air is warm, the Arctic fox sheds.* It adapts when its environment changes. Have you spotted the Arctic fox yet?

Lots of other animals blend in with their environments. Can you spot them?

*sheds gets rid of hair

What Do You Think?

What do these animals do to survive in their environments?

Wildlife in the City

by Eliza Redding • illustrated by Deborah Melmon

"Look at this!" Tara yelled. "A falcon lives on top of the Glenford Building! How did it get there? How will it survive?"

Max always had his fact book on wildlife. He pulled it from his pocket and read these facts.

Fact: Animals can adapt to new environments and find ways to survive.

Fact: Some animals make homes outside their usual places.

Fact: Lots of animals make their homes on city lampposts and buildings.

Tara and Max wanted to explore wildlife in their neighborhood. Tara cut out the story and placed it in her pocket.

The Daily
FALCON SPOTTED ON SKYSCRAPER

OWL
WHALE

"Max, I spot tracks in the mud. What animal do you think these prints came from?"

Max flipped pages in his book. "This picture matches these tracks. A wild rabbit made these prints."

"Why does it live in the city?" Tara asked. Max read more facts.

Tara and Max followed the prints to a hole
behind shrubs.

"Is it in there?" Tara asked.

"It could be," Max answered. "I once read that rabbits dig and hide in holes. They like to be protected by trees and grass."

"What does it eat, Max?"

"Rabbits munch on plants, twigs, and tree bark," Max said.

All of a sudden Tara looked up. "Max, look up at that bird!"

"It must be the falcon that sits on the skyscraper!"

"Why does it live on the skyscraper?" Tara asked. Max read these facts.

Fact: Some wildlife such as birds live in places a long way up.

Fact: Places like these help them spot and hunt animals.

FALCONS

Tara pulled out the falcon story. "Cliffs are their usual homes. That must be why they like skyscrapers! Falcons hunt birds and animals like rabbits. Falcons can spot things from far away."

"This falcon must have spotted the rabbit that made these prints," Max said.

"Look! It is leaving," said Tara. "It must be moving from this city to explore another place."

"Falcons can glide in the air for hundreds of miles at a time," Max said.

"The falcon will survive!" Tara said.

"The rabbit will too!" said Max.

What Do You Think?

How did the wildlife in this story adapt to city life?

Animal Champs

These animal champs are fast, strong, and they live a long time!

Fast Diving

This whale dives fast! Think about your size. What if 137 kids like you stand one on top of another in the water? This whale can dive past all of you in one minute. That is about 183 yards straight down!

Strong Lifting

This bug is very strong. It is a rhinoceros beetle. It can carry as many as 850 insects just like it! Can you think of any other animal that can lift that much?

Trick Flying

This little bird can move five different ways. It can go up, down, backward, forward, and side to side. And it flaps its wings about 5,000 times a minute!

Strong Building

A spider spins a web of thin silk. This silk is stronger than some metal. It can stretch too. Most spiders can make a big web in an hour.

Long Living

A clam can live a long, long time! It lets us know its age. Look at the rings on this shell. A clam grows a ring every 12 months. How many rings does this clamshell have?

218 219 220

4 for 2 Do

Word Play

What are the missing letters? The clues can help.

1. p___k   You can play ball or swing and slide here.
2. c___n   This is a yellow vegetable.
3. b___n   Cows and horses live in this building.
4. f___m   You can find crops and animals here.

Making Connections

Imagine you are one of the animals you read about. With a partner, take turns telling how you will be safe from other animals. Use these words: *environment, protect, survive, adapt,* and *wildlife.*

On Paper

Draw an outdoor environment. Show animals that live in that environment. Write about how the animals adapt.

Answers to Word Play: ar (park); or (corn); ar (barn); ar (farm)

Good Choices

Contents

Good Choices

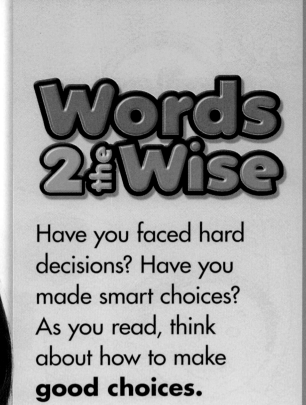

Words 2 the Wise

Have you faced hard decisions? Have you made smart choices? As you read, think about how to make **good choices.**

Solving Problems

Fred and June were tossing a stuffed cat back and forth.
"Can you catch this one?" asked June. June tossed the cat
far up in the air.

Fred jumped up and grabbed it. "I got it!" he said.

Then Fred pitched the stuffed cat to June. He pitched it harder than ever!

As soon as it left Fred's hands, he saw the problem coming. "Catch it, June!" yelled Fred.

Fred put his hands over his eyes. He did not want to watch. He hoped that June would catch it!

35

June jumped and stretched. She had to grab it! But it slipped through June's hands. She missed it!

The stuffed cat crashed into Mom's expensive vase. The kids' eyes were fixed on the vase.

"Oh, no," said June. "What did we do?"

"We have a big problem," said Fred.

"I have an idea," said June. "We can hide it in the tan chest."

"I think we have two choices," said Fred. "We can hide Mom's vase, or we can tell Mom what happened. Then we can save our allowance and buy a new vase."

Fred and June can use some good advice. What decision do you think is best?

Rosa Parks
Takes a Stand

by Allison Katen

When Rosa Parks was a girl, black people and white people did not live by the same rules. Many rules at that time did not let blacks do the same things as whites. These rules were based on people's skin color.

Rosa Parks

One rule did not let black children and white children attend the same schools. Another rule did not let blacks get the same jobs as whites. There was even a rule about sitting on a bus. These rules were not fair. They were a problem.

But in 1955, Rosa Parks decided to take a stand that would help change one rule.

Rosa rode the bus to her job every day. She gave a dime for bus fare like everyone. But a rule said that blacks had to let whites sit first. Rosa followed this rule. Sometimes she got to sit, and sometimes she had to stand.

But one day the bus was almost filled. Rosa sat in one of the last spots on the bus.

A white man got on Rosa's bus. The driver told her to get up so the man could sit in her spot. Rosa remembered her grandfather's advice. He said, "You are just as good as anyone."

Then Rosa made a brave choice. She decided not to give up her place. But Rosa ended up behind bars for that decision.

Rosa Parks broke the law. For that she went to jail.

At that time, Martin Luther King Jr. was working to change rules like the one Rosa broke. He hoped people would look at each other for who they were, not for their color. He wanted fair rules for people of every race. Martin and Rosa knew it would be hard to change these rules. But lots of people supported them.

Many people worked with Martin Luther King Jr. and Rosa Parks to bring change.

Martin decided to object to the bus rule in Rosa's city. Rosa and others objected with him. Black people and some whites stopped riding buses. They helped one another get to school and to jobs.

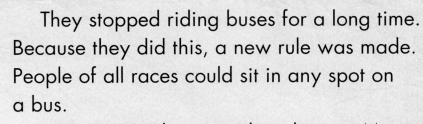

They stopped riding buses for a long time. Because they did this, a new rule was made. People of all races could sit in any spot on a bus.

Soon more rules started to change. Martin and Rosa did not give up. They worked for better rules that were fair for all people.

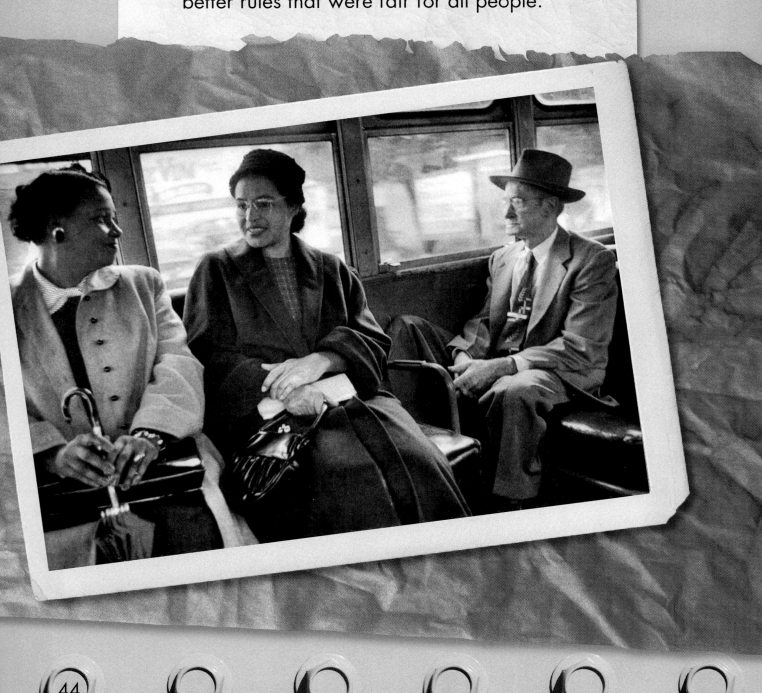

People admired what Rosa and Martin did to get rules changed. Rosa Parks decided to take a stand by herself. Her decision not to give up her place on the bus was a brave act. It helped people's lives. Now people of all races can have better lives.

What Do You Think?

What was life like in the United States before Rosa Parks and Martin Luther King Jr. took a stand? What was it like after?

Curt's Big Decision

by Emile Von Wagman • illustrated by Elena Selivanova

One hot summer day a flock of birds were taking a dip in a garden pond. Gertrude stopped to admire herself. "Look at my plumes.* They are beautiful!" she said.

"Your plumes are nice," said Gertrude's pals. "But we have nice plumes too."

"Not as nice as mine," bragged Gertrude. "Mine are perfect!"

*__plumes__ feathers

After some time, the flock's top bird spoke up. "Gertrude," she said. "The members of this flock have made a decision. We are tired of your bragging. And we do not like rude birds!" At that, the flock flapped their wings and off they went.

Gertrude turned up her nose. "That flock will miss me. They will be back."

Just then a rabbit hopped out of the ferns. Curt hopped over to Gertrude.

"Gertrude," he said, "I have a problem. My fur is not shining. Will you shine it up for me?"

"Not now, Curt," Gertrude snapped. "Can you not see that I am fixing my plumes?"

Curt felt hurt. Where were Gertrude's manners?

Curt told his pals what had happened.

"Is it any surprise?" asked Frog. "Gertrude will not help anyone. Gertrude is rude."

"I am planning a party," Curt said. "I had planned to invite Gertrude. But now I wonder if that is such a smart idea."

Curt had cards for his party. "Do not invite Gertrude," his pals told him.

Curt stopped to think. Gertrude *was* rude. But would he be rude if he did not invite her?

Curt had a big decision to make. Should he take his pals' advice, or should he invite Gertrude?

You Are Invited

What: A Party

When: Today at 6:00 p.m.

Where: At the Garden Pond

Curt thought long and hard. Then he decided. He had better not invite Gertrude.

Later that day, the animals were getting set for Curt's party. Gertrude saw them and felt hurt. And she missed her flock.

Then Curt saw Gertrude. Had he made a bad choice? He checked his pocket. He felt one more card. "I am going to invite Gertrude after all," he told his pals.

"But Gertrude is rude," chirped Cricket.

"Do you want that rude bird at your party?" Frog blurted.*

*****blurt** to say something without thinking

Curt handed Gertrude the last card. Gertrude read it and smiled. "Thanks," she said. "But first I had better help shine your fur."

"Will you fix us up for Curt's party too?" the animals asked.

"Yes," Gertrude said. She patted her plumes. "I will make you just as beautiful as I am!"

What Do You Think?

What was Gertrude like at the beginning of the story? What was she like at the end of the story?

Answers from Ally

Read Together

Do you make good choices? Advice from an expert can help!

Dear Ally,
    Some big kids at school pick on my best friend. I am afraid to tell them to stop. What can I do?
        Small Kid with a Big Problem

Dear Small Kid,
    Get your friend to tell an adult about the problem. It's not safe to keep it a secret. Offer to go with him.
        Ally

Dear Ally,
    My friend and I found a wallet by the curb. It had ten dollars in it. Can we split the money? What should we do?
                    Just Wondering

Dear Just Wondering,
    Take the wallet to your mom, dad, or a police officer. Ask that person to help you find out who lost it. The person who lost it will be glad to get it back.
                    Ally

4 You 2 Do

Word Play

It's rhyme time! Find the rhyming words to finish these silly sentences.

> girl   herd   churn   germ   hurt
> stern   skirt   firm   twirl   bird

A ripped part of a dress is a ___ ___.

A young woman who spins around is a ___ ___.

A bunch of animals with wings is a ___ ___.

A business that makes flu bugs is a ___ ___.

A strict tool for making butter is a ___ ___.

Making Connections

Pretend you are Rosa Parks, Gertrude, Curt, or one of Curt's pals. In a small group, act out each one's answer to this question: Should you treat others as they treat you?

On Paper

Rosa Parks and Curt made brave choices. Write to tell why you think they made the choices they did.

Answers for Word Play: hurt skirt, twirl girl, bird herd, germ firm, stern churn

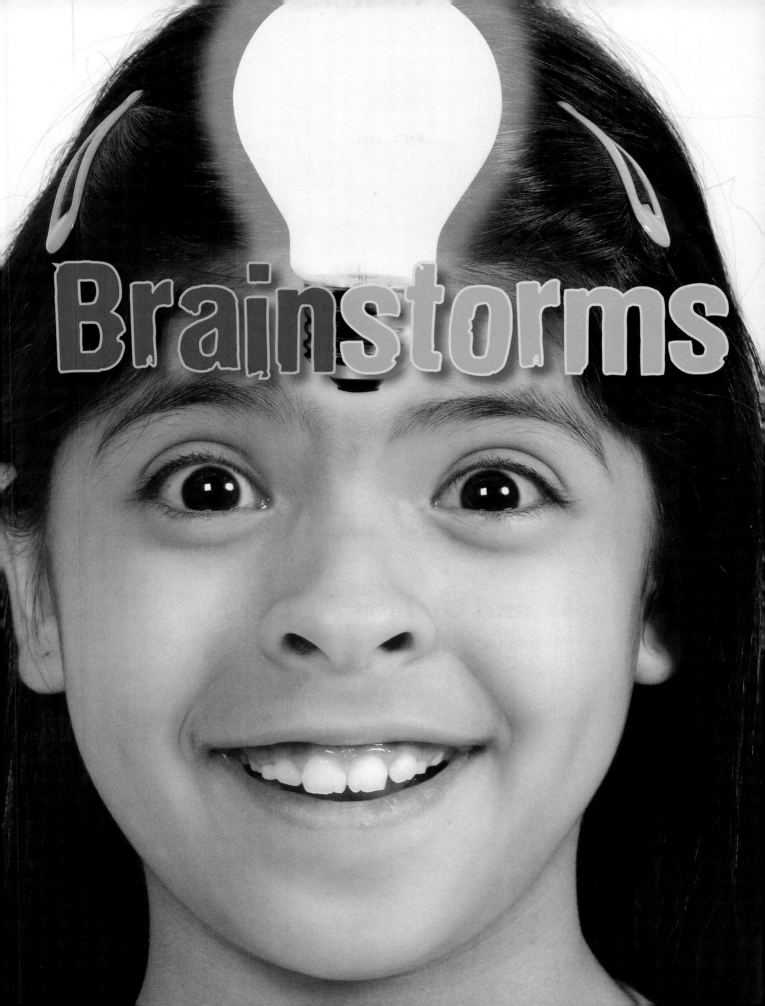

Brainstorms

Contents

Brainstorms

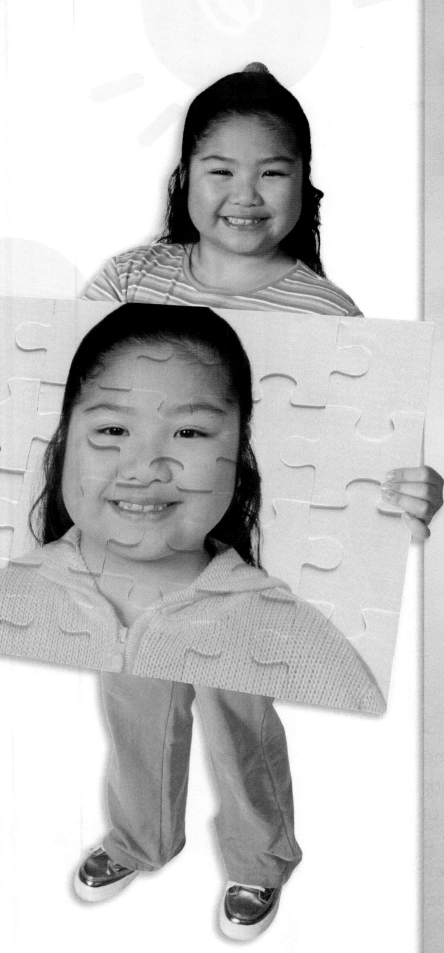

Words 2 the Wise

How do inventors come up with their ideas? It all begins with **brainstorms.** Do you have a great idea? You can be the next great inventor!

Bright Ideas

How do inventors get ideas for an invention? Ideas pop up in many places. Inventors can get an idea at the park or on a bus. They can get ideas at home or at school.

When you get an idea, write it on paper. Then think. Is it new? Will it solve a problem? Will it make life better?

Inventors get good ideas! Ideas can be for machines, games, toys, puzzles, and ways to make life better.

It takes lots of time to plan an invention. Inventors work hard to make an invention that lots of people can use.

When an idea pops up, inventors jot notes or make sketches. They may even make the first one. Then people can see the invention and can test it.

At one time, cars and rubber bands were brand new inventions!

Think about computers and cars. These inventions started with an idea.

The wildest idea can make a great invention! Just think about this wild idea—notes that stick. These notes were newer and better than what was used before. Now everybody uses them.

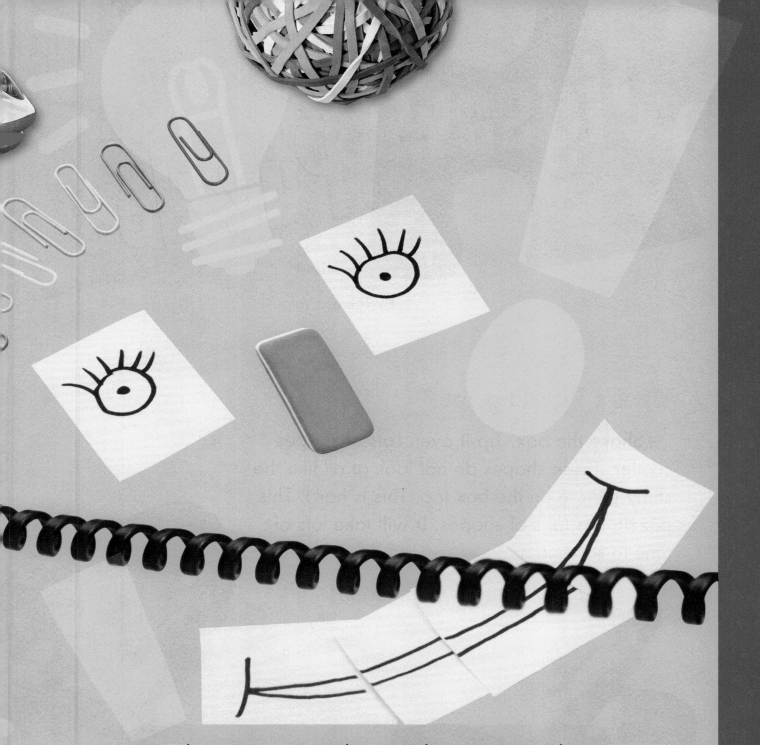

The Internet started as an idea. Now it is the fastest way to send notes, learn facts, and find games and puzzles.

People can use the Internet to get ideas for inventions. Can they think of a newer, better invention? Will it work? Will it fail? Time will tell.

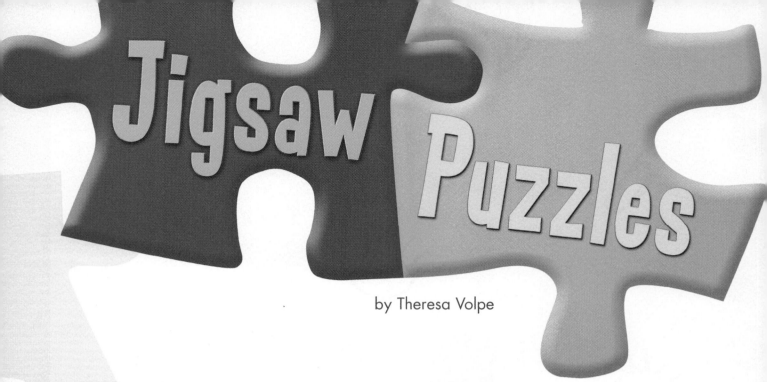

Jigsaw Puzzles

by Theresa Volpe

What's Puzzling You?

Shake the box. Tip it over. Lots of shapes scatter. These shapes do not look at all like the shiny picture on the box top. This is hard. This puzzle has tons of shapes. It will take lots of time to solve it.

You spot a pattern. Some shapes have straight sides. Others do not.

You spot two red shapes. Those shapes fit. How lucky! Then you try another red shape. It fits! Soon you can see the top corner. It is a success!

These puzzle pieces are making a picture!

A Puzzling Invention

People have been solving these puzzles for a long time. Who invented them?

John Spilsbury made maps. He also made an invention to help kids learn. He put a map on a hard block. Then he cut the hard block into shapes. He invented puzzles in 1767.

U.S.A. MAP

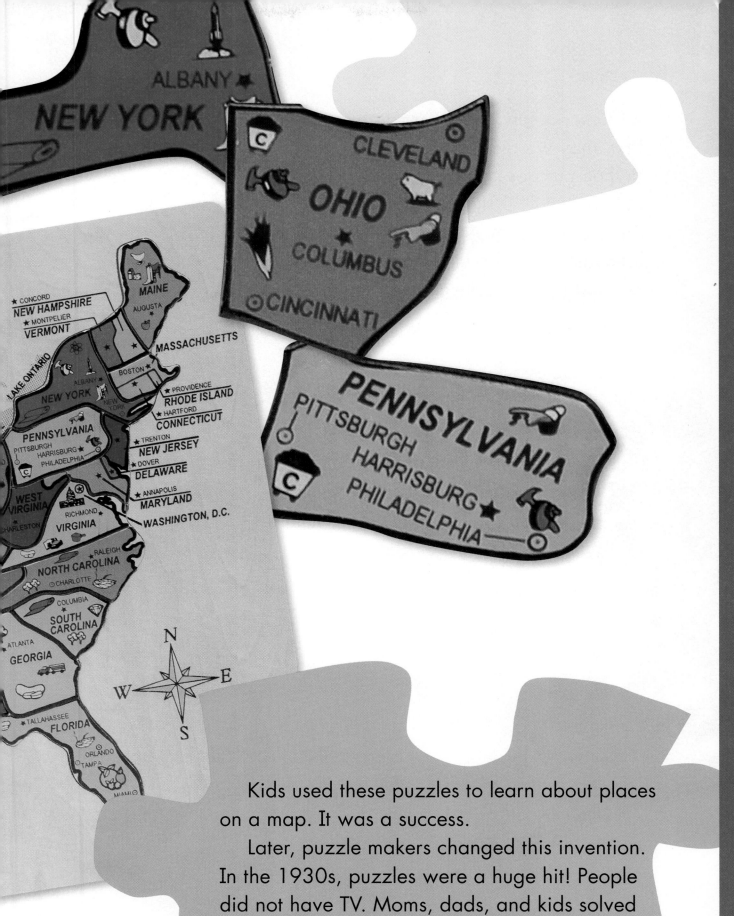

Kids used these puzzles to learn about places on a map. It was a success.

Later, puzzle makers changed this invention. In the 1930s, puzzles were a huge hit! People did not have TV. Moms, dads, and kids solved these puzzles for fun.

A Better Puzzle

As time passed, people made puzzles better. At first, they were cut one shape at a time. Back then puzzles cost five dollars. That was lots of cash in 1908!

Then machines were invented. Machines cut shapes faster. Now puzzles do not cost very much, and more people can buy them.

A FEAST IN FAIRYLAND

Puzzles have changed in many ways since the 1760s.

In the past, shapes did not lock together. This made it hard to complete a puzzle. In the past, puzzles did not come with pictures. Solvers had to complete an entire puzzle to get the solution. Today, we can use the box top for help.

69

In the past, puzzles were flat. Solvers wanted them to be harder. Puzzle makers made 3-D puzzles for them to try.

These puzzles can stand up. Fit together, these shapes make homes, globes, and sports cars! These puzzles are hard, but it is fun trying to solve them.

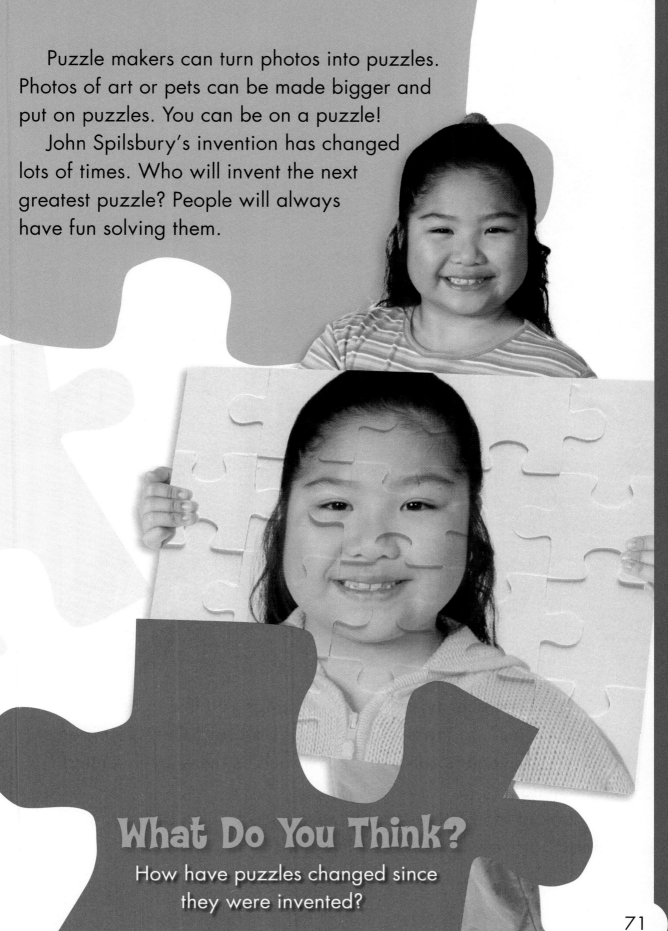

Puzzle makers can turn photos into puzzles. Photos of art or pets can be made bigger and put on puzzles. You can be on a puzzle!

John Spilsbury's invention has changed lots of times. Who will invent the next greatest puzzle? People will always have fun solving them.

What Do You Think?

How have puzzles changed since they were invented?

Gadgets and Gizmos

by Jamie A. Schroeder

Have you ever wished that the things you like to use were made better? Do the brakes on your bike fail? Does your pen run dry? Inventors solve problems such as these by inventing new things.

Look at the pictures on the next pages. Think about the hints. Can you name these inventions?

Earl Dickson's wife cut her finger. He wanted to help. Earl made a sticky strip with a pad of cotton on it. He placed the strip around her finger. It kept dirt from getting in. His solution worked!

Most kids have a box filled with these at home. They come in many sizes and shapes. Can you name these sticky things?

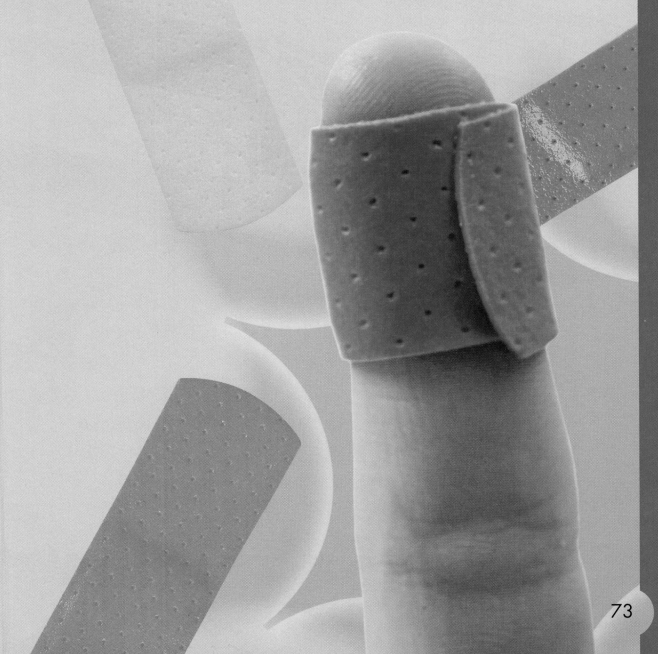

A person can sit in this. It can fly through the sky. It has a nose and two wings like a bird. It does not have legs. It uses gas like a car.

The first time a man rode in this invention was on December 17, 1903. It did not fail, but it did not fly very far.

Inventors worked to make this invention better. Now it is much bigger and faster. It can take people from place to place in much less time. It can even fly around the world! What is it?

Douglas Engelbart wanted to make his computer work faster. He wanted to make it easy to use. He invented a solution for these problems.

His invention fit in his hand. It had two wheels and a cord. He placed it on a pad and used his hand to slide it.

In the 1960s, many people used this invention with their computers. It has gotten much better. Now many of them can work without cords. Your computer at home or school uses this invention too. What is it?

For a long time, people used an invention with a cord to communicate with others. They could not step farther than the length of the cord. Martin Cooper had an idea to make it better.

He made a handy invention that did not have a cord. People did not have to stand or sit in one place to use it. What is it?

Inventors try hard to make new things to solve problems. Some inventions work well. Others fail. Inventors try to make these inventions better. What invention would you like to make better?

What Do YOU Think?

Pick one of the inventions you read about.
Tell how it has made life better.

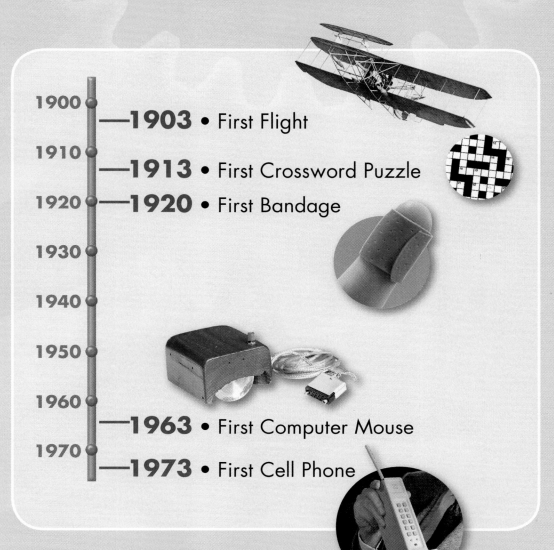

1900
1910
1920
1930
1940
1950
1960
1970

1903 • First Flight

1913 • First Crossword Puzzle

1920 • First Bandage

1963 • First Computer Mouse

1973 • First Cell Phone

Silly Solutions

Taking a dog for a run is simple, right? You put a leash on the dog, open the front door, and start running. But what kind of invention could give a dog exercise without its owner? Maybe the invention would look like this.

The Bow Wow Track

1. A chicken lays an egg.
2. The egg rolls down. It hits a car.
3. The car pulls a rope that is hooked to a pail of water.
4. The pail tips. Water spills on a sleeping kangaroo.
5. The kangaroo wakes up. It jumps up and down on a pump.
6. The pump fills a balloon with air.
7. The balloon rises up. It hits the On switch.
8. The dog starts running.

4 YOU 2 DO

Word Play

You just invented a robot! Complete these rhymes to tell about it.

I named my robot Willy

because he is so _____.

He has a friend named Marty.

They want to have a _____.

These robots are so sly.

They have wings to help them _____.

Willy and Marty flew up in the sky.

If they don't come back, I think I will _____.

Making Connections

You read about different types of inventions. Which one is your favorite? Why is that invention important to you?

On Paper

If you could invent something to solve a problem, what would it be? Draw a picture and write about it.

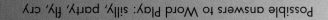

Possible answers to Word Play: silly, party, fly, cry

YOUR FAIR SHARE

Contents

YOUR FAIR SHARE

Words 2 the Wise

How can a kid be responsible? Read to find out how you can do **your fair share.**

Being Responsible

Kids around the world try hard to be responsible. These kids like doing the right thing. They help take care of things at home, in school, and in their community. How can a kid be responsible?

Danny and his pals have puppies, bunnies, and kittens. It is their responsibility to take care of them. These kids must wash and dry their pets. They must give them things to eat and fresh water to drink. They must let their pets run and jump. They have fun with them too.

Cammy's responsibility is helping little kids. The kids are her reading buddies. First she reads them the funniest stories she can find. Then her buddies take turns. Cammy tries her hardest to help kids when they get stuck. Cammy is proud to help these kids learn to read.

Danny and Cammy are responsible kids. They help care for people and things around them. They are proud that they can help. Danny's puppy is well and happy. Soon Cammy's buddies will be reading well.

Do you help care for people or things around you? Be proud. You are responsible!

Take Care of You

by Lisa Wong

Responsible kids do lots of things to help. Responsibility is taking care of people and things around you. It is helping with chores at home and at school. It is doing a job that you can be proud of. But responsibility does not end there!

You are responsible for you! Responsible kids eat things that are good for their bodies. They get lots of exercise* and plenty of rest. And they make sure that their bodies are kept spick-and-span.

*exercise (EK-ser-syz) moving your body to make it stay strong and healthy

Munch and Crunch!

Our bodies get energy* from things we eat. This energy gets us going.

Responsible kids pick the right things to eat. They drink water and three glasses of milk every day. For lunch and dinner, they fill up on yummy things like these.

*__energy__ (EN-er-jee) the power to move, work, or play

Responsible kids make the right choices about snacks too. They pick grapes, berries, or nuts for snacks rather than candy. They drink milk or water rather than soft drinks.

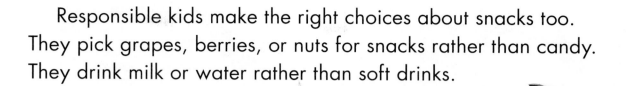

Get Moving!

Responsible kids exercise for an hour every day. They run and jump and stretch to build strong bodies. Swimming, jumping rope, and skating are fun ways to get moving. Doing chores is a smart way to exercise. Making a bed, raking leaves, or washing a car gets your body moving.

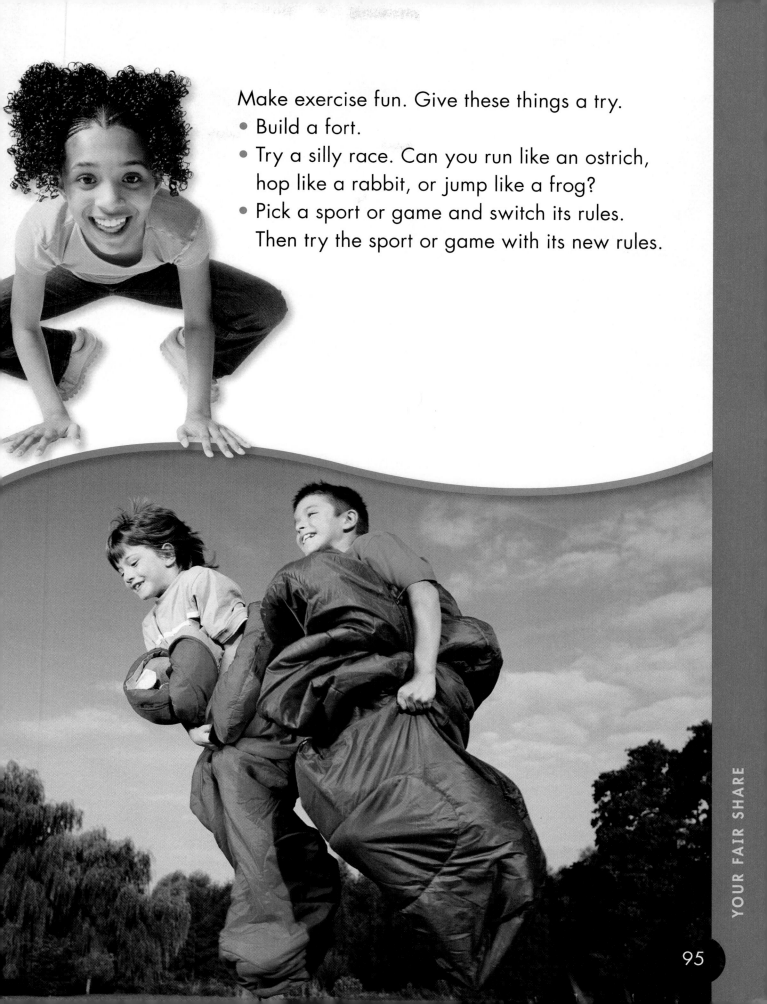

Make exercise fun. Give these things a try.
- Build a fort.
- Try a silly race. Can you run like an ostrich, hop like a rabbit, or jump like a frog?
- Pick a sport or game and switch its rules. Then try the sport or game with its new rules.

Put on the Shine!

Germs are all around us. Responsible kids protect their bodies by scrubbing to a shine. Splish, splash! They wash their hands often to get off dirt and germs. Brush, brush! Responsible kids like nice white smiles too.

Eat right, exercise, scrub the germs away, and get plenty of rest. You will not go wrong if you do these things. Only you live in your body. Take care of it! It just takes responsibility!

What Do You Think?
Tell how you can be responsible for yourself each day. Start when you wake up. End when you go to bed.

THE HOME RUN CHAMP

by Jean Rogers • illustrated by Mick Reid

"Strike two!" yelled Abby.

"Rats!" Will muttered.* He stepped back from the plate and stretched his arms. "I still get one more try," he said.

"Pitch me a nice one!" Will yelled to Justin as he got set to swing.

*__mutter__ to say words with your lips partly closed

Smack! Will started to run. He felt proud of that hit.

"Look at that thing fly!" cried Abby.

"Home run!" Justin yelled as Will sprinted past first base.

All of a sudden there was a crash—a BIG crash. Justin and Abby ran to have a look.

YOUR FAIR SHARE

"Will! Come see this!" Abby yelled.

Will sprinted over to her. His eyes got big as they rested on the house next to his. "Yikes!" he cried. "I broke that glass!"

A man came out on his porch. "Run!" Abby and Justin cried. "Do not let him see us!"

Will was tempted to run. But he knew that running was the wrong choice. He had to take responsibility for breaking the glass. That was the right thing to do.

Will made his way to the porch. Will's tummy started to hurt as he went up the steps.

The man held out his hand. "I am Rod Jones," he said. Then he grinned.

Will was shocked. Mister Jones was not mad. "I am Will Cortez," Will said. "I broke your glass."

"Will Cortez," Mister Jones said, "you are one splendid* hitter! And you are quite responsible as well."

*splendid very good

102

Will felt the happiest he had felt all day. He liked Mister Jones. They sat down on the porch steps.

"Would your pals like to sit with us?" Mister Jones asked.

Justin and Abby crept out of the shrubs. They had scratches all over their arms.

103

Will turned to Mister Jones. "I will give you money for that glass," he said. "My allowance is not much. But I will save every penny of it."

"I have a better idea," Justin said. "We can ask people to hire us for odd jobs. Then we can earn money faster."

That summer was the hottest and driest ever. But that fact did not stop Will, Justin, and Abby. They worked hard to earn money for Mister Jones's glass. And Mister Jones gave them a hand. He was their best and happiest customer!

What Do You Think?
How did Will feel at the beginning of the story? in the middle? at the end?

Mind These Rules!

Do not slurp spaghetti
Or put ketchup on your toast.
Do not bring a snake to dinner
Or eat up all the roast.

Do not dress dogs in feathers
Or spill a jar of glue.
Do not burp when someone's talking
Or paint Mom's toenails blue.

Do not take mice to school
Or put them on a chair.
But take a turn to make a rule
That's sillier, if you dare.

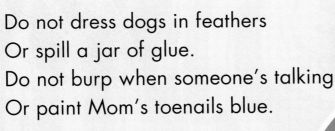

107

4 YOU 2 DO

Word Play

Can you say this tongue twister fast?

Tongue Twister
Penny is proud of painting perfect purple pictures.

Make up tongue twisters using these words. Then ask a pal to say them fast.

proud

right

wrong

responsible

responsibility

Making Connections

Will showed Mister Jones that he was responsible. How did Will show that he was responsible about himself too?

On Paper

You read about responsible kids. Now make up a kid who is <u>not</u> responsible. What would that kid do?

PROBLEMS for PLANTS and ANIMALS

Contents

PROBLEMS for PLANTS and ANIMALS

Words 2 the Wise

How do plants and animals survive extreme weather? How do they protect themselves from enemies? Read to find out about **problems for plants and animals.**

Problems for Animals

What is the climate like where you live? Climate is what the weather is like most of the time. Some places have an extreme climate. It may be very hot. Or it may be very cold. Animals in these places must find clever ways to survive.

The Desert

The desert is a place with an extreme climate. By day, the sun makes this place hot, hot, hot. But when the sun sets, it gets chilly.

This kangaroo rat hides in holes under the hot sand.

By day, desert animals must get shelter from the hot sun. Some stay in the shade. Others hide in holes under the hot sand. When the sun sets, these animals come out to hunt. The desert comes to life when it is dark!

This kit fox comes out to hunt at the end of the day.

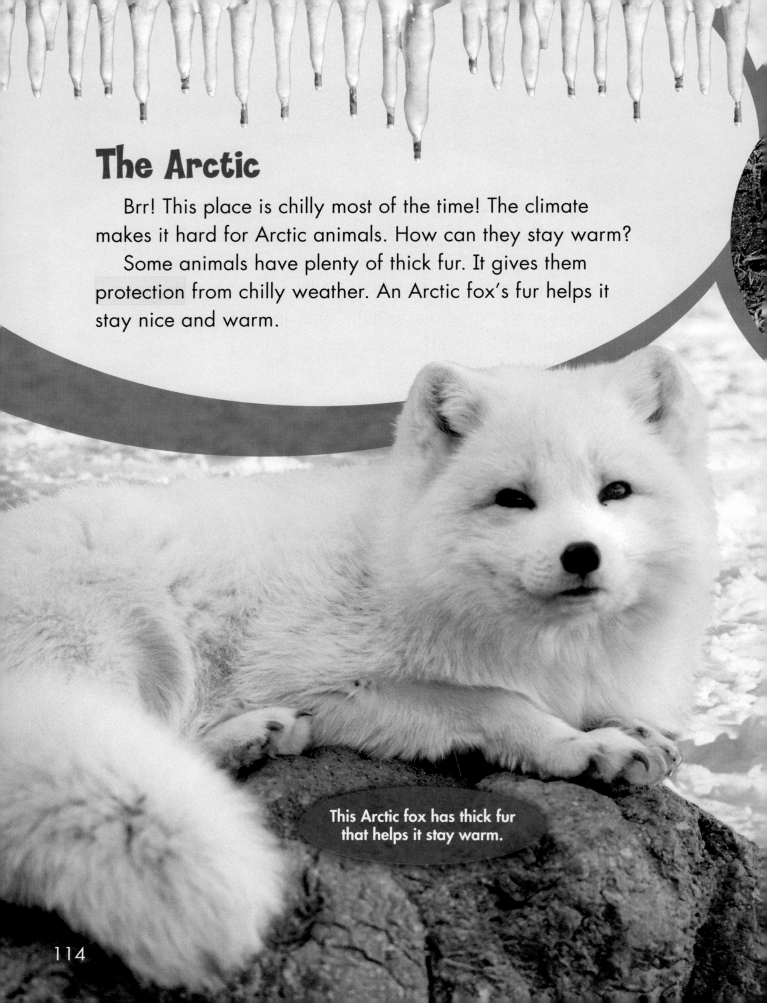

The Arctic

Brr! This place is chilly most of the time! The climate makes it hard for Arctic animals. How can they stay warm?

Some animals have plenty of thick fur. It gives them protection from chilly weather. An Arctic fox's fur helps it stay nice and warm.

This Arctic fox has thick fur that helps it stay warm.

This Arctic squirrel naps all winter long and comes out in spring.

Some Arctic animals do not like this chilly weather. Before winter, they go into their snug homes. They nap all winter and come back out in spring.

Other animals leave home to get away from the Arctic climate. Before winter, they move to a much warmer place. They stay until spring. Then they move back home!

Caribou (KAR-uh-boo) move to a warmer place before winter.

Into the Deep

by Chuck Consodine

Many animals and plants live in Earth's seas. Many live in tide pools, the places where sea and shore meet.

Life in the sea is not always easy. Plants and animals must find shelter and things to eat. They must also get protection from other plants and animals that will harm them.

SEA LAYERS

The sea has layers, or zones. The sun warms the top layer. Many plants and animals live in this sunny zone. But the sun's rays do not shine all the way into the sea. Far below the surface, it is dark. Only special animals can survive in such an extreme place!

SUNLIT ZONE

SCHOOL OF FISH

LIFE IN THE SUN

Most sea animals live in the top layer. What sort of problems do they have? They must stay safe from other animals that will eat them!

One kind of fish stays safe by hiding in what looks like a plant. But its hiding place is not a plant. It is another animal—a sea anemone (uh-NEM-uh-nee)! Most fish can not touch a sea anemone because it can harm them.

Only the clownfish is safe from the anemone's stings.

ANEMONE

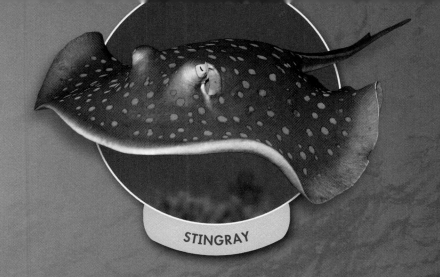

STINGRAY

Many animals move in groups to stay safe. Some little fish swim under big fish for protection. But the puffer fish is different. It just gets bigger if it is afraid. It puffs up like a balloon! Then other animals become afraid of the puffer fish and it stays safe!

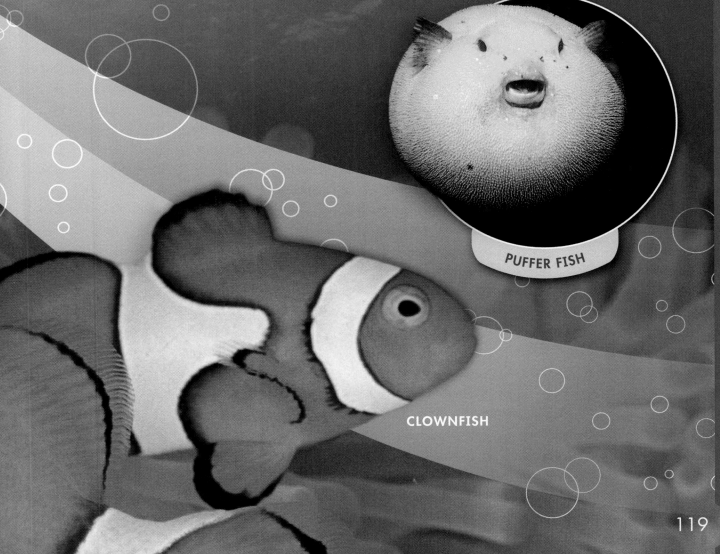

PUFFER FISH

CLOWNFISH

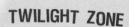
TWILIGHT ZONE

DARK ZONE

SWORDFISH

DOWN INTO THE DARK

Water in the next layer down is darker.
Some fish that live here have big eyes to help
them see better. The sun may not shine in this
layer, but some animals do! They shine to find
their way, to get food, and for protection.

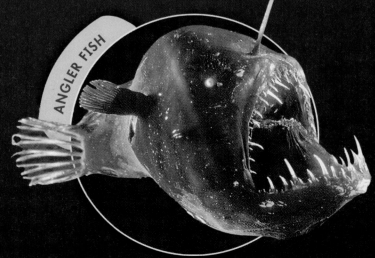
ANGLER FISH

Another fish sees the
light of the angler fish
and follows it. Then
SNAP! The angler fish
gets dinner!

You can not see way down to the bottom layer. If you could, you would see that some strange animals live in this dark, dark place!

There are vents, or openings, on the bottom of the sea. Hot gas comes out of them. A kind of worm lives on these vents. This worm has adapted to live in an extreme place.

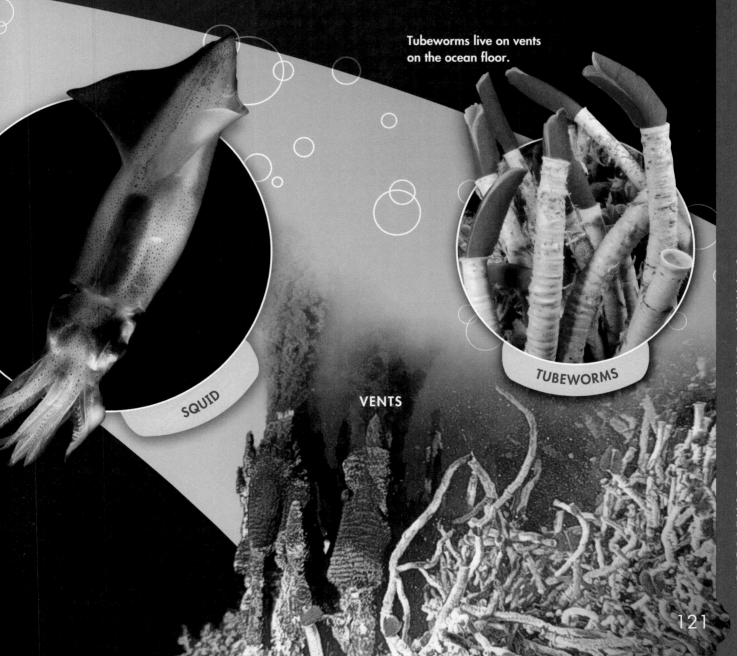

Tubeworms live on vents on the ocean floor.

SQUID

VENTS

TUBEWORMS

CRAB

SUNLIT ZONE

TWILIGHT ZONE

DARK ZONE

TIDE POOLS

Some animals live on shore next to the water. This place is always changing. Every day, water moves toward land and away from it. There may be a lot of water at one time and not much at another time. These changes are called *tides*.

A tide pool is a pocket of water left when the tide goes out.

SEA URCHIN

Tides may make pockets of water on shore. Some plants and animals in these places cling to sand or rock. This way they do not get washed away when the tide comes in or goes out. Other animals just walk away. They can live in water or out of it! They have adapted to live where there are tides.

SEAGRASS

STARFISH

WHAT DO YOU THINK?

What are some ways that plants and animals survive in the sea?

Why Giraffes Have Long Necks

a folk tale retold by Gayle Howard • illustrated by Tim Bowers

Long ago, Giraffe (juh-RAF) and her family had short necks, short tails, and short hair with dark spots. They lived on the grassy plains of a distant land. Trees and shrubs gave them shelter. And there were lots of plants for the animal families to eat.

124

"I like this place," Giraffe told Hippo. "The climate is not extreme. It is never too hot or too cold."

"Yes," said Hippo. "The weather is fine. And we have lots of grass to eat."

Soon more and more families moved to this happy place. But then things began to change.

"There are too many of us and not enough to eat," Zebra complained. "The grass and plants are all gone!"

"What can we do?" asked Gazelle.

Giraffe spotted new leaves in the tree tops. "Maybe we can get those leaves," she said. "They look yummy."

The others laughed. "We can not get them. They are way, way up! We are not that big!"

"I think we can solve this problem if we work together," said Giraffe. And she explained her plan.
"It may work," Hippo said. "I will help."
"So will we," added the others.

127

"Get up on my back," Hippo said. One by one, the friends got up on Hippo's back. Giraffe was last. She sat on top and picked leaves for everyone.

"Thank you, Giraffe," said Gazelle as he munched on leaves.

"Yes!" the others said. "We must do this every day!" And so they did.

But one day, there was a big, big wind. The animals swayed this way and that. "Look out!" yelled Hippo.

Those below Giraffe began to slip. One by one, they fell out from under her. "Yikes!" exclaimed Giraffe as her head got trapped in branches.

"Giraffe's head is stuck!" cried Hippo.

Sure enough, Giraffe hung from the tree branches. "What can we do?" asked Zebra.

"Stretch your legs, Giraffe!" Hippo yelled. Giraffe did. But her legs did not touch the grass.

"Stretch more!" Gazelle cried. But still Giraffe hung from the tree.

"Grab her legs," Zebra yelled. So they grabbed and tugged . . . and tugged . . . and tugged.

At last, Giraffe's legs touched the grass. "Look at her long, long neck!" Hippo exclaimed. "Giraffe is as tall as the tree!"

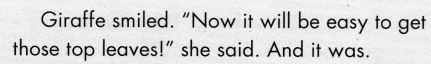

Giraffe smiled. "Now it will be easy to get those top leaves!" she said. And it was.

"We want long necks too!" said Giraffe's family. So they stretched and tugged until their necks were just as long. And that is why giraffes today have long necks.

What Do You Think?

Was Giraffe's plan a good way to solve the problem? Can you think of another solution?

131

Plant Power!

Many plants have special ways of taking care of themselves. Come take a look. But don't get too close!

Venus's Flytrap

Any bug that flies too close to this plant gets a big surprise. **SNAP! WHAP!** The flower snaps shut, and the bug becomes fast food!

Sundew

Bugs that land on this plant never leave. Why? The plant is gooey and the bugs stick to it. Then the plant has a ready meal whenever it needs it!

Sensitivity Plant

Talk about touchy! When this plant is touched, its leaves curl up and it appears wilted. This protects it from animals that might try to eat it. When the danger is over, the plant springs back to life!

Eastern Skunk Cabbage

PHEW! What's that smell? This plant gives off a stinky odor to keep animals from eating it. That's why *skunk* is part of its name!

Cactus

A desert has very little rain. But this desert plant has a way to make the most of every drop. Its stem and branches collect and store water. Then its thick, waxy "skin" keeps the water inside. How refreshing!

133

Word Play

Choose the word that best answers each riddle.

extreme   climate   weather

shelter   protection

1. I tell what it feels like outside. I may be warm today. I may be cool tomorrow. You can hear about me on the news. What am I?

2. I am a place, like a house, that protects you. What am I?

3. I am more than usual. I can describe a place that is very hot or very cold. What am I?

Making Connections

How do plants and animals survive in extreme climates?

On Paper

You read about interesting plants and animals. Write about the one you think is most interesting. Tell why you think as you do.

Glossary

a • dapt (ə dapt′), *VERB.* to change something to fit different conditions; adjust: *They will adapt to the weather in Florida.* **a•dapt•ed, a•dapt•ing.**

ad • vice (ad vīs′), *NOUN.* an opinion about what should be done: *My advice is that you study more.*

choice (chois), *NOUN.*
1 something picked out from a group: *I had to make a choice as to which book to read.*
2 the power or chance to choose: *I have my choice between a radio and a camera.*
3 person or thing you picked or chose: *Sitting in this seat on the bus is my choice.*

cli • mate (klī′ mit), *NOUN.* the kind of weather a place has: *Climate includes conditions of temperature, rainfall, and wind.*

de • cide (di sīd′), *VERB.* to choose something: *I usually decide to stay home when I do not feel well.* **de•cid•ed, de•cid•ing.**

de • ci • sion (di sizh′ ən), *NOUN.* the act of making up your mind about something: *I have not yet made a decision about buying that bicycle.*

a in hat	ō in open	sh in she
ā in age	ȯ in all	th in thin
â in care	ô in order	ҭн in then
ä in far	oi in oil	zh in measure
e in let	ou in out	⌈ a in about
ē in equal	u in cup	⎪ e in taken
ėr in term	u̇ in put	ə = ⎨ i in pencil
i in it	ü in rule	⎪ o in lemon
ī in ice	ch in child	⌊ u in circus
o in hot	ng in long	

en•vi•ron•ment (en vī′ rən mənt), *NOUN.* everything in the world that surrounds a living thing: *Plants will grow in an environment that has enough light and water.*

ex•treme (ek strēm′), *ADJECTIVE.* much more than usual; very great: *She drove with extreme caution during the snowstorm.*

fail (fāl), *VERB.* to not be able to do something; not succeed: *Will her idea work, or will it fail?* **failed, fail•ing.**

in • ven • tion (in ven′ shən), NOUN.
a new thing that someone makes
or thinks of: *The light bulb was a
wonderful invention.*

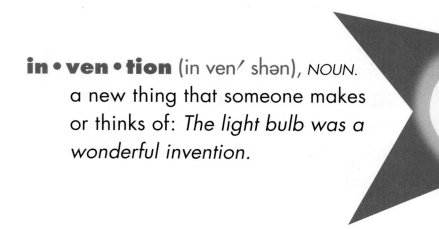

prob • lem (prob′ ləm), NOUN.
1 a question or situation, especially a difficult one: *I have
a problem seeing in the dark.*
2 something you have to work out the answer for: *I have
another math problem to do.*

pro • tect (prə tekt′), VERB. to keep someone or something safe
from harm or danger; defend; guard: *An umbrella can
protect you from rain.* **pro•tect•ed, pro•tect•ing.**

a in hat	ō in open	sh in she
ā in age	ȯ in all	th in thin
â in care	ô in order	ŦH in then
ä in far	oi in oil	zh in measure
e in let	ou in out	⎧ a in about
ē in equal	u in cup	⎪ e in taken
ėr in term	u̇ in put	ə = ⎨ i in pencil
i in it	ü in rule	⎪ o in lemon
ī in ice	ch in child	⎩ u in circus
o in hot	ng in long	

pro•tec•tion (prə tek′ shən), NOUN.

1 the act of keeping someone or something safe from harm; defense: *We have a large dog for our protection.*

2 someone or something that prevents damage: *A hat offers protection from the sun.*

proud (proud), ADJECTIVE. feeling pleasure or satisfaction in something that you have done: *I am proud to have been chosen class president.*

puz•zle (puz′ əl),

1 NOUN. a game that you work out for fun: *Help me put the pieces of this puzzle together.*

2 VERB. to make it hard for someone to understand something; confuse: *How the cat got out puzzled us.* **puz•zled, puz•zling.**

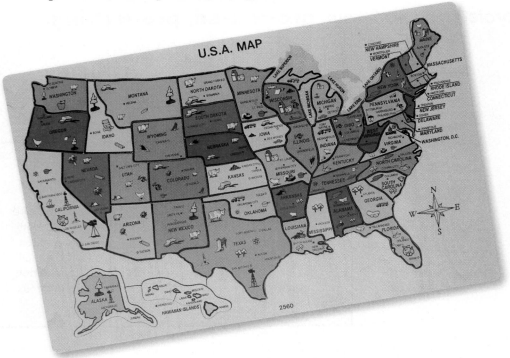

a	in hat	ō	in open	sh	in she
ā	in age	ô	in all	th	in thin
â	in care	ô	in order	ŦH	in then
ä	in far	oi	in oil	zh	in measure
e	in let	ou	in out		a in about
ē	in equal	u	in cup		e in taken
ėr	in term	u	in put	ə =	i in pencil
i	in it	ü	in rule		o in lemon
ī	in ice	ù	in rule		u in circus
o	in hot	ch	in child		
		ng	in long		

re·spon·si·bil·i·ty (ri spon/ sə bil/ ə tē), NOUN.
1 the act or fact of being responsible; duty: *We agreed to share responsibility for planning the birthday party.*
2 someone or something that you are trusted with: *Keeping my room clean is my responsibility.*
PL. **re·spon·si·bil·i·ties.**

re·spon·si·ble (ri spon/ sə bəl), ADJECTIVE.
1 expected to take care of someone or something: *You are responsible for getting your homework done.*
2 able to be trusted; reliable: *The teacher chose a responsible student to take care of the class pet.*

right (rīt), ADJECTIVE.
1 good; just; lawful: *She did the right thing when she told the truth.*
2 correct; true: *She had the right answer on the test.*
3 fitting; proper: *Say the right thing at the right time.*

shel·ter (shel′ tər), NOUN. something that covers or protects you from weather, danger, or attack: *Some people use tents for shelter when they are camping.*

so·lu·tion (sə lü′ shən), NOUN. the process of solving a problem or explaining a mystery: *It was hard to think of a solution for the problem.*

solve (solv), VERB. to find the answer to something; clear up; explain: *Did the detective solve the mystery?* **solved, solv·ing.**

sur·vive (sər viv′), VERB. to continue to live or exist; remain: *We need food and water to survive.* **sur·vived, sur·viv·ing.**

weath • er (weŦH′ ər), NOUN. the conditions of the air outside at a certain place and time: *The weather is cold and windy.*

wild • life (wīld′ līf′), NOUN. wild animals and plants: *The campers saw many kinds of wildlife.*

wrong (rông), ADJECTIVE.
1 not the way it should be or not right: *Stealing is wrong.*
2 not true; not correct: *She gave the wrong answer.*

a	in hat	ō	in open	sh	in she
ā	in age	ò	in all	th	in thin
â	in care	ô	in order	ŦH	in then
ä	in far	oi	in oil	zh	in measure
e	in let	ou	in out		a in about
ē	in equal	u	in cup		e in taken
ėr	in term	u̇	in put	ə = { i in pencil
i	in it	ü	in rule		o in lemon
ī	in ice	ch	in child		u in circus
o	in hot	ng	in long		
ô	in hot	ng	in long		

Acknowledgments

Illustrations

Cover: Deborah Melmon; **2, 28, 29** Pete Whitehead; **3, 98–105** Mick Reid; **20–27** Deborah Melmon; **34, 36** Mernie Gallagher Cole; **46–53, 138** Elena Selivanova; **58, 80, 82** Bill Ledger; **110, 124–130** Tim Bowers; **132** Bob Dacey; **142** Patricia Keeler.

Photographs

Every effort has been made to secure permission and provide appropriate credit for photographic material. The publisher deeply regrets any omission and pledges to correct errors called to its attention in subsequent editions.

Unless otherwise acknowledged, all photographs are the property of Pearson Education, Inc.

Photo locators denoted as follows: Top (T), Center (C), Bottom (B), Left (L), Right (R), Background (Bkgd)

Cover: (CR) ©Paul Barton/Corbis, (BR) ©Royalty-Free/Corbis, (CL) Galen Rowell/Corbis; **1** (CL) ©Rubberball Productions; **2** (BR) Eric Glenn/Getty Images; **3** (BR) ©blickwinkel/Alamy Images, (BR) ©Royalty-Free/Corbis, (T) Getty Images, (BR) Rubberball Productions/Getty Images; **5** (C) Jose Luis Pelaez/Corbis; **6** (T) Jose Luis Pelaez/Corbis, (TR) Pete Atkinson/Getty Images; **7** (C) Jean - Michel Foujols/Jupiter Images; **8** (T) Blickwinkel/Alamy Images, (CR) Joe McDonald/Corbis, (BR) Juniors Bildarchiv/Alamy Images; **9** (TR) Blickwinkel/Alamy Images, (T) Buddy Mays/Corbis; **10** (T) Pete Atkinson/Getty Images; **11** (T) Firefly Productions/Corbis; **12** (C, Bkgd) Jeffrey L Rotman/Corbis; **13** (C) Kevin Schafer/Corbis; **14** (TC) Joe McDonald/Corbis, (Bkgd) Kevin Schafer/Corbis; **15** (T, Bkgd) Kevin Schafer/Corbis; **16** (Bkgd) Anna Grossman/Getty Images, (C) Linda Lewis/Jupiter Images; **17** (Bkgd) Anna Grossman/Getty Images, (TC) Roger Eritja/Alamy Images; **18** (C) Eberhard Hummel/Corbis, (Bkgd) Jim Zuckerman/Corbis; **19** (T, Bkgd) Galen Rowell/Corbis; **31** (C) Charles C Place/Getty Images; **32** (T) Frank Micelotta/Getty Images, (Bkgd) Jupiter Images; **38** (BC) Corbis, (TL) Jim West/Alamy Images, (Bkgd) Jupiter Images; **39** (C) Bettmann/Corbis; **40** (Bkgd) Jupiter Images, (C) Time & Life Pictures/Getty Images; **41** (C) gene Herrick/AP/Wide World Photos; **42** Jupiter Images, (C) Time & Life Pictures/Getty Images; **43** (C) Bettmann/Corbis; **44** (C) ©Don Cravens/Time & Life Pictures/Getty Images, Jupiter Images; **45** (BC) Frank Micelotta/Getty Images; **54** (BL) Eric Glenn/Getty Images, (TR) Jupiter Images; **57** (T) H. Prinz/Corbis; **58** (TR) Gary Ombler/©DK Images; **60** (TR) ©David McGlynn Photography, (L) Getty Images, (BR) Stockbyte Platinum/Getty Images; **61** (TC) ©Royalty-Free/Corbis, (BR) Getty Images; **62** (TR) Martyn Goddard/Corbis; **63** (TC) ©Corbis; **68**

(BC) ©Michael O'Mara Books/The Art Archive, (BR) ©Nicolas Sapieha/Poggio Petroio Dog Collection/The Art Archive, (BL) SuperStock; **69** (T) ©Judith Miller/Cobwebs/©DK Images, (BR) Gary Ombler/©DK Images, (C) Geoff Brightling/©DK Images; **72** (BR) ©Royalty-Free/Corbis, (C) fStop/Getty Images, (CL) Getty Images; **74** (C) ©Underwood & Underwood/Corbis; **75** (TR, BC) ©Royalty-Free/Corbis; **76** (CL) ©SRI International; **77** (B) JLP/Deimos/Corbis; **78** (BL) Big Cheese Photo; **79** (CR) ©Royalty-Free/Corbis, (BC) ©SRI International, (TR) ©Underwood & Underwood/Corbis, (BR) Liz Mangelsdorf/Corbis; **83** (C) Getty Images; **84** (TR) BananaStock, (B) Don Mason/Corbis; **85** (C) Steve Lyne/Getty Images; **87** (TR) IT Stock Int'l/Jupiter Images, (CR) Steve Lyne/Getty Images; **89** (BR) Comstock Images, (CR) Denis Felix/Getty Images, (TC) Michael Pole/Corbis; **90** (TC) Comstock Images, (B) Getty Images; **91** (B) Bob Elsdale/Getty Images; **92** (C) BananaStock, (TR) Getty Images; **93** (BL) ©Royalty-Free/Corbis, (BR) BananaStock, (TR) Getty Images; **94** (T, B) Getty Images; **95** (TL) ©Rubberball Productions, (B) Tim Hall/Getty Images; **96** (T) ©mylife photos/Alamy, (L) ©Royalty-Free/Corbis, (BL) Hein van den Heuvel/Corbis, (BR) Jennie Woodcock/Corbis; **97** (B) Zen Sekizawa/Getty Images; **106** (CL) ©BananaStock/SuperStock, (TL) ©Iconotec/Alamy, (B) Donna Day/Getty Images; **107** (BR) BJ Formento/Corbis, (T) Don Mason/Corbis, (BC) Getty Images; **108** (CR) Rubberball Productions; **109** (C) ©Wayne Lynch/PhotoLibrary Group, Inc.; **110** (CR) ©Julie Mowbray/Alamy Images; **111** (C) ©Paul Souders/Getty Images, (CL) ©Sigrid Dauth (Travel Germany 2005)/Alamy Images; **112** (C) ©Dinodia Dinodia/PhotoLibrary Group, Inc., (BL) ©Joe McDonald/Getty Images; **113** (B) ©Julie Mowbray/Alamy Images; **114** (C) ©Mark Wallace/Alamy, (C) ©Staffan Widstrand/Nature Picture Library, (T) Getty Images; **115** (C) ©Charles George/Visuals Unlimited, (BR) Photolibrary Group, Inc.; **116** (TL) ©Mark Jones/Minden Pictures, (C) ©Paul Souders/Getty Images; **118** (C) ©Birgitte Wilms/Minden Pictures, (C) ©Comstock Images/Jupiter Images, (T) ©Martin Strmiska/Alamy; **119** (T) ©blickwinkel/Alamy Images, (CR) ©Fred Bavendam/Minden Pictures; **120** (C) ©Comstock Images/Jupiter Images, (T) ©Norbert Wu/Minden pictures/National Geographic Image Collection, (B) ©Image Quest Marine; **121** (CR) ©Al Giddings, (C) ©Dante Fenolio/Dante B. Fenolio, MS, Ph.D./Atlanta Botanical Garden Center for Conservation, (B) Verena Tunnicliffe/University of Victoria, BC, CA; **122** (T) ©Bob Elsdale/Getty Images, (C) ©Dennis Frates/Alamy Images, (CR) ©Guillen Photography/UW/Canada/Vancouver/Alamy; **123** (B) ©Wolfgang Polzer/Alamy Images, (C) Jeff Foott/Getty Images; **136** (B) ©Don Cravens/Time & Life Pictures/Getty Images; **137** (T) Bryan and Cherry Alexander/Alamy Images; **139** (T) H. Prinz/Corbis; **143** (C) Kevin Schafer/Corbis.

144